GW00706044

BESTEST MUM EVER

summersdale

BESTEST MUM EVER

Summersdale Publishers Ltd
46 West Street
Chichester
West Sussex
PO19 1RP
UK

www.summersdale.com

Printed and bound in China

ISBN: 978-1-84953-131-3

Substantial discounts on bulk quantities of Summersdale books are available to corporations, professional associations and other organisations. For details contact Summersdale Publishers by telephone: +44 (0) 1243 771107, fax: +44 (0) 1243 786300 or email: nicky@summersdale.com.

To: ....

From: ....

A woman is like a teabag.
You can't tell how strong
she is until you put her
in hot water.

Nancy Reagan

I couldn't live without
my music, man.
Or me mum.

Robbie Williams

I'm a mother with two small children, so I don't take as much crap as I used to.

Pamela Anderson

I am extraordinarily patient, providing I get my own way in the end.

Margaret Thatcher

If evolution really works,
how come mothers only
have two hands?

Milton Berle

Any mother could perform the jobs of several air traffic controllers with ease.

Lisa Alther

THINGS THAT MUMS CAN DO WITH ONE HAND TIED BEHIND THEIR BACK

☆ Organise the week ahead for the entire family - assorted pets included

☆ Know when their children are up to no good

☆ Pull Schumacher-style car manoeuvres when parking the car at a supermarket

☆ Hang out a bumper load of washing
   while ironing the last lot

☆ Change a duvet cover

☆ Bake a batch of themed culinary
   treats for any occasion

☆ Get the old family photo albums out and
   open to the baby pictures before your new
   flame has even sat down

☆ Make it all better

MUM

The hand that rocks the cradle usually is attached to someone who isn't getting enough sleep.

John Fiebig

I got my figure back after giving birth. Sad, I'd hoped to get somebody else's.

Caroline Quentin

There is no way to be a
perfect mother, and
a million ways to
be a good one.

Jill Churchill

We have charts, maps and lists on the fridge, all over the house. I sometimes feel like I'm with the CIA.

Kate Winslet

I feel incredibly lucky and blessed, but I do sometimes feel like that *Exorcist* lady!

Kate Beckinsale

If men had to have babies,
they would only ever
have one each.

Diana, Princess of Wales

A mother is one to whom you hurry when you are troubled.

Emily Dickinson

If love is sweet as a flower, then my mother is that sweet flower of love.

Stevie Wonder

YOU KNOW YOU'RE A MUM WHEN...

☆ ... you count the number of chips on each child's plate to keep the peace at mealtimes

☆ ... your dream date is Fireman Sam

☆ ... you realise you now sound like your own mother

☆ ... you can rustle up a feast to rival Nigella from leftovers in the fridge

☆ ... you always look slightly bedraggled while your child looks immaculate

☆ ... you can carry five bags of shopping, your child and your child's bike across town without getting out of breath!

☆ ... you automatically ignore all white clothes in the shops – you don't do white anymore!

☆ ... you find yourself telling anyone who'll listen just what a genius your child is

MUM

My mom is literally a part of me. You can't say that about many people except relatives, and organ donors.

Carrie Latet

You've got to love your mum more than yourself, although I do come a very close second.

Simon Cowell

For most exhausted
mums, their idea of
'working out' is a good,
energetic lie-down.

Kathy Lette

Mothers are inclined to feel limp at 50... because the children have taken most of her stuffing to build their nests.

Samantha Armstrong

An ounce of mother is worth a ton of priest.

Spanish proverb

My mother made a brilliant impression upon my childhood life. She shone for me like the evening star.

Winston Churchill

Making the decision to have a child is... forever to have your heart go walking around outside your body.

Elizabeth Stone

When you are a mother,
you are never really alone
in your thoughts.

Sophia Loren

THINGS THAT MAKE MUMS CRY

☆ First burp, first word, first steps - first anything, really!

☆ Seeing her child off on the first day of school - extra tissues needed for when it's university

☆ Watching her little Oscar winner in the school play - and seeing the video again and again afterwards!

☆ A home-made card or painting (to go straight up on the kitchen noticeboard)

☆ Reading a school report – whatever its content

☆ Getting breakfast in bed on Mother's Day – who cares if the toast is cold?

☆ When someone else does the washing up for a change (this probably doesn't happen very often)

☆ Seeing her scruffy teenager all smartened up for the school dance – amazing what a bit of soap and water can do, isn't it?

☆ Weddings – it doesn't matter who's getting married!

Sweater, n.: garment worn by child when its mother is feeling chilly.

Ambrose Bierce

Until I got married,
when I used to go out,
my mother said goodbye
to me as though I
was emigrating.

Thora Hird

It seems to me that my mother was the most splendid woman I ever knew.

Charlie Chaplin

She would have despised the modern idea of women being equal to men. Equal, indeed! She knew they were superior.

Elizabeth Gaskell, *Cranford*

Children and zip fasteners
do not respond to force...
except occasionally.

Katherine Whitehorn

My mother had a great
deal of trouble with
me, but I think
she enjoyed it.

Mark Twain

Mother is far too clever to understand anything she does not like.

Arnold Bennett

A mother's heart is the child's classroom.

Henry Ward Beecher

THINGS THAT ONLY A MUM CAN TEACH

☆ Religion – 'You'd better pray that comes out in the wash...'

☆ Medical Science – 'Don't cut off your nose to spite your face.'

☆ Logic – 'Because I said so.'

☆ Mathematics – 'I'm going to give you until the count of three: one... two...'

☆ Probability - 'You're going to be late for school if you don't leave now.'

☆ Recycling - 'I'll have your guts for garters if you don't behave!'

☆ Performance Art - 'I feel like I'm talking to a brick wall.'

☆ Philosophy - 'Who do you think you are?'

I refuse to admit that I am more than 52, even if that does make my sons illegitimate.

Nancy Astor

Children are a great comfort in your old age. And they help you reach it faster, too.

Lionel Kaufman

Mother – that was the bank where we deposited all our hurts and worries.

T. DeWitt Talmage

The patience of a mother might be likened to a tube of toothpaste - it's never quite all gone.

Anonymous

My mother's great... She could stop you from doing anything, through a closed door even, with a single look.

Whoopi Goldberg

She was of the stuff of which great men's mothers are made. She was... hated at tea parties, feared in shops, and loved at crises.

Thomas Hardy describing
Bathsheba Everdene in
Far From the Madding Crowd

No one knows like a woman how to say things that are at once gentle and deep.

Victor Hugo

A smart mother makes often a better diagnosis than a poor doctor.

August Bier

SECRET SKILLS THAT ONLY MUMS KNOW

☆ How to speak Baby

☆ How to interpret squiggly drawings: 'What a lovely house! Oh, it's a dog – how beautiful!'

☆ How to make a meal that looks like a smiley face

☆ How to get everyone washed, dressed and out of the house before 9 a.m.

⭐ How to make a box into a
robot/car/spaceship

⭐ How to mend toys, clothes and
broken hearts

⭐ How to frighten off the monsters
under the bed

⭐ How to make home feel like home

To a child's ear,
'mother' is magic
in any language.

Arlene Benedict

I will accept lots of things, but not when someone insults my mum, the nicest person in the world.

Andy Murray

The phrase 'working mother' is redundant.

Jane Sellman

Raising a kid is
part joy and part
guerrilla warfare.

Ed Asner

She never quite leaves her children at home, even when she doesn't take them along.

Margaret Culkin Banning

There is only one pretty child in the world, and every mother has it.

Chinese proverb

A man's got to do
what a man's got
to do. A woman must
do what he can't.

Rhonda Hansome

Motherhood is not for the faint-hearted. Frogs, skinned knees and the insults of teenage girls are not meant for the wimpy.

Danielle Steel

AWARDS FOR THE 'BESTEST MUM EVER'

☆ Bravery in the Face of Gross Things

☆ Culinary Genius

☆ Queen of Solutions

☆ Extraordinary Alertness After a Night of No Sleep

☆ Royal Order of Organisational Prowess

☆ Most Patient Parent

☆ Kindest Nurse

☆ Best Hand Holder

☆ The Golden Car-Key Award for Chauffeuring

☆ Most Attentive Listener

☆ Cheerleader in Chief

Sing out loud in the car
even, or especially,
if it embarrasses
your children.

Marilyn Penland

The strength of motherhood is greater than natural laws.

Barbara Kingsolver

Children keep us in check. Their laughter prevents our hearts from hardening.

Queen Rania of Jordan

Some are kissing mothers and some are scolding mothers, but... most mothers kiss and scold together.

Pearl S. Buck

Child-rearing myth #1:
labour ends when
the baby is born.

Anonymous

Before I got married, I
had six theories about
bringing up children. Now,
I have six children and
no theories.

John Wilmot,
2nd Earl of Rochester

Women, you know,
do seldom fail
To make the stoutest
men turn tail.

Samuel Butler, 'Hudibras'

There are only two things
a child will share willingly
– communicable diseases
and his mother's age.

Dr Benjamin Spock

THINGS IN MUM'S HANDBAG

☆ Hand sanitiser

☆ Spare pair of socks

☆ Factor 50 sun cream

☆ A seemingly endless supply of
tissues and plasters

☆ Emergency chocolate supplies

 Safety pins

☆ Digital camera

☆ Hairclips

☆ Mittens on a string

☆ Foldable anorak

☆ Umbrella

☆ A notebook and lots of
   pens and pencils

Motherhood in all its guises and permutations is more art than science.

Melinda M. Marshall

God could not be everywhere, so he created mothers.

Jewish proverb

A mother is not a person to lean on, but a person to make leaning unnecessary.

Dorothy Canfield Fisher

I think my life began with
waking up and loving
my mother's face.

George Eliot, *Daniel Deronda*

Working mothers are
guinea pigs in a scientific
experiment to show that
sleep is not necessary
to human life.

Anonymous

A suburban mother's role is to deliver children obstetrically once, and by car for ever after.

Peter De Vries

There's nothing like
a mama-hug.

Adabella Radici

She may scold you for little things, but never for the big ones.

Harry S. Truman

YOU NEVER GET REALLY CROSS WITH ME, EVEN WHEN...

☆ ... I come home covered in mud from head to toe

☆ ... I leave my wet towel in a heap on the bathroom floor

☆ ... I use your designer wardrobe as my dressing-up box

☆ ... I forget that it's my turn to empty the dishwasher

☆ ... I wake you up complaining of nightmares before demanding a space in the bed

☆ ... I never remember to turn the lights off when leaving a room

☆ ... I drink orange juice from the carton

☆ ... I sleep in until noon and then only grunt in acknowledgement as I pass you in the kitchen

MUM

A father's goodness
is higher than the
mountain, a mother's
goodness deeper
than the sea.

Japanese proverb

Only mothers can think of the future – because they give birth to it in their children.

Maxim Gorky

Parenthood: the state of being better chaperoned than you were before marriage.

Marcelene Cox

You will always
be your child's
favourite toy.

Vicki Lansky

The heart of a mother is a deep abyss at the bottom of which you will always find forgiveness.

Honoré de Balzac

There was never a great
man who had not a great
mother - it is hardly
an exaggeration.

Olive Schreiner

A mother is the truest friend we have.

Washington Irving

That's the 'right' thing, I'm thinking – when you love someone more than you love yourself. That's what I think about my mum.

Cheryl Cole

All that I am or ever hope to be, I owe to my angel Mother.

Abraham Lincoln

A little girl,
asked where her
home was, replied,
'Where mother is.'

Keith L. Brooks

YOU'RE THE BESTEST MUM BECAUSE...

☆ ... you take me shopping until I've found exactly the right thing to wear

☆ ... you always tell me I can do it

☆ ... you listen to all my stories – and you remember them

☆ ... you know just how to cheer me up

☆ ... you're my favourite person to natter with over a cup of tea

☆ ... you always have time to talk

☆ ... you know how to get red wine stains out of my best party outfit

☆ ... you're always there for me

☆ ... you've never resigned, despite having lots of reasons to!

Thank you for being...

THE BESTEST
MUM EVER!

www.summersdale.com